Eat This Book

STUDY GUIDE

Eat This Book

STUDY GUIDE

Eugene H. Peterson & Peter Santucci

WILLIAM B. EERDMANS PUBLISHING COMPANY
GRAND RAPIDS, MICHIGAN / CAMBRIDGE, U.K.

Published 2006 by
Wm. B. Eerdmans Publishing Co.
2140 Oak Industrial Drive N.E., Grand Rapids, Michigan 49505 /
P.O. Box 163, Cambridge CB3 9PU U.K.
www.eerdmans.com
Printed in the United States of America

11 10 09 08 07 06   7 6 5 4 3 2 1

ISBN-10: 0-8028-3263-6 / ISBN-13: 978-0-8028-3263-4

Eat This Book is published in association with the literary agency of Alive
Communications, Inc., 7680 Goddard Street #200, Colorado Springs, CO 80290

Contents

CONTENTS

Contents

Preface

This is a book about a book about a book — a guide to a book about reading the Bible. My hope is that using this study guide will help you and your community do exactly what Eugene Peterson set out to do when he wrote *Eat This Book* — namely, read and meditate on and pray and live the book this is all about, the Scriptures.

As Peterson notes in his book, we use words to hide just as much as to reveal, to lie as much as to tell the truth. This is true of both what we write and what we say. Because of that, I think of this study guide as an archaeologist's tool. Each question is meant to gradually and determinedly scrape away at us and at Scripture, peeling back the accumulated layers that have obscured us and the Word of the Lord.

You can use this tool effectively on your own, but it is best used in a community of Christians. There's a certain level of honesty that can be reached only when we answer questions aloud in front of people who know us — honest speech becomes a truth event in which we articulate things that we may not have intended to say but that change us as a result. Silent thoughts that don't escape the mind rarely do that.

This study guide can be used for a seven-session or a nine-session group study. It is currently formatted for a nine-session study, with each chapter of *Eat This Book* receiving its own attention. However, chapters 2 and 6 are fairly short and can easily be combined with the immediately following chapters. Still, my recommendation is the more leisurely nine-week study. After all, this isn't fast food we're eating here; it's Holy Scripture!

Each session has a summary of the section covered — usually a single chapter. I've included this for the sake of the group leader(s). You may or may not want to read this aloud before the group discussion. One problem with reading summaries aloud in small groups is that such summaries can lead to laziness, as when I was in eighth grade and read CliffNotes on *Moby Dick* instead of the complete novel.

Along with questions for interaction, I've included quotations to consider. Eugene Peterson is eminently quotable, and I've had to restrain myself with the number of quotations included. (My wife was helpful in that process.) At times we need questions to spark our interaction, but at other times, simply reading a powerful and representative quotation is more effective in generating interaction.

But remember, this guide includes a lot of quotations and questions. Make sure you consider the amount of time you have available for conversation and discussion before you pick which ones to use. Simply starting with the first question or the first quotation and trying to get through them all would be a mistake, unless you're using this guide for personal study. No group I know could have any depth of interaction while dealing with all the quotations and questions.

Each session also has a suggested activity. It will tangibly enhance your group time, engaging the group physically with the ideas expressed in the chapter. Some of the activities require advance preparation, so please make sure you allot enough time to prepare for those. Some activities are better done before the discussion time, while others are better done during or afterward. Again, putting time and thought into preparation is essential to getting the most out of your study group.

I've also ended each session with a prayer based on Psalm 119. Psalm 119 is the great, mammoth psalm (176 verses) that meditates on Scripture from almost every possible angle. The first line of each verse in each eight-verse section starts with the same Hebrew letter as the psalm works its way through the Hebrew alphabet. Each time your group moves from study to prayer, focus on one section from this psalm. In small-group prayer times, the focus generally moves almost completely from Scripture to our individual lives. Psalm 119 can help keep the two together.

So, take the eight verses from each section and write them out on separate pieces of paper, distributing them to the people in your group as you move to prayer. If you have fewer than eight people, you can either give people more than one verse or just use as many verses as there are people in the group. The text from Eugene Peterson's translation *The Mes-*

sage is included with each session, but feel free to use whichever translation makes the best sense for you and your small group.

Encourage those who feel less comfortable with verbal prayers in a group setting to simply read aloud their verse in a prayerful way, letting the psalmist give them words to speak. But encourage the group as a whole to begin with the psalmist's words and then add their own, both as they praise God for the gift of Scripture and as they add their own prayers of request, thanksgiving, love, and confession.

If you're using this study guide with a group that's been meeting together for a while, you probably have an established rhythm and way of interacting. If you're fairly new at this or are willing to explore a different shape for your time together, here's how our community groups operate (the groups I had in mind when I wrote this guide). It's fairly simple. We gather for a meal. The sharing of food makes it much easier to share our lives. Church-related talk isn't permitted during meals. Talk about anything and everything else is encouraged. After the meal, we have our discussion time. Next, we take a break for dessert. And then we gather again for prayer. That's all. It's not a foolproof technique, but it's a basic rhythm that makes sure that not only are we discussing the passage or book for that evening, but we're also engaging each other as friends and praying for each other.

Whatever shape your group takes, make sure to take time to pray together, bringing before God your daily experiences and your engagement with Scripture. Hopefully, the conversations coming out of your discussions of the questions in this guide will give you plenty to pray over. Again, consider using sections from Psalm 119 as a launching point for your praying.

And speaking of conversations, Peterson has subtitled his book *A Conversation in the Art of Spiritual Reading*. Scripture reading is first and foremost a conversation with God, but it is best done in conversation with other Bible readers.

You might be interested to know that my writing of this study guide was also done in Scripture-shaped conversations — with Eugene, with First Presbyterian Church of Lebanon, with my covenant group, and always with my wife, Charlene, who got rid of the weaker questions in this guide and who always sends me back to God in prayer and Scripture.

Transfiguration of the Lord 2006   PETER SANTUCCI

Preface and Chapter One

(pp. x-xii and 1-11)

Summary

The Bible is one of the most respected books in the world, if not the most respected. It has been honored and put on a pedestal for centuries. It has been read devoutly by millions. However, the elevation of the Scriptures has so often left a gap between them and our lives. But reading the Scriptures is to be entwined with the living of our lives because it ties our lives to God. Scripture reading is simply "letting Another have a say in everything we are saying and doing" (p. xii). Nothing is more simple. Or more difficult.

We don't read the Bible to get God into our world but to get ourselves into God's world.

Karl Barth (borrowing from Plato's analogy of the Cave) likened reading Scripture to stepping from a dark, constrained warehouse into the wide-open, sun-lit world outside. Here's how Peterson puts it: "When we open the Bible . . . we enter the totally unfamiliar world of God, a world of creation and salvation stretching endlessly above and beyond us. Life in the warehouse never prepared us for anything like this" (p. 7).

In Scripture, Bible reading is referred to in several places as "eating" the book, taking it in completely and not just in pieces, ingesting it so that it becomes a part of our very being. As we "read with our entire life," our goal is "participatory reading, receiving the words in such a way that they become interior to our lives, the rhythms and images becoming practices of prayer, acts of obedience, ways of love" (p. 10). This isn't easy, because it requires us to encounter God and submit our whole lives to him, but it is truly nourishing.

Obstacles to a participatory reading of Scripture are the use of words as propaganda (to manipulate) or as information (to control). "Propaganda works another person's will upon us," says Peterson, "and commodification of language reduces both those who speak it and those who listen to it also to commodities" (p. 10).

Key Term

Lectio divina: "often translated 'spiritual reading,' reading that enters our souls as food enters our stomachs, spreads through our blood, and becomes holiness and love and wisdom" (p. 4).

Quotations to Consider

"What is neglected is reading the Scriptures formatively, reading in order to live. . . . In order to read the Scriptures adequately and accurately, it is necessary at the same time to live them. Not to live them as a prerequisite to reading them, and not to live them in consequence of reading them, but to live them *as* we read them" (pp. xi-xii).

"Holy Scripture is the source document, the authoritative font, the work of the Spirit that is definitive in all true spirituality" (p. 4).

"What I mean to insist upon is that spiritual writing — *Spirit*-sourced writing — requires spiritual reading, a reading that honors words as holy, words as a basic means of forming an intricate web of relationships between God and the human, between all things visible and invisible" (p. 4).

"Meanwhile Barth, in his small out-of-the-way village, was writing what he had discovered, the extraordinary truth-releasing, God-witnessing, culture-challenging realities in this book, the Bible" (p. 5).

Barth wrote numerous books that "would convince many Christians that the Bible was giving a truer, more accurate account of what was going on in their seemingly unraveling world than what their politicians and journalists were telling them" (p. 5).

"We open this book [the Bible] and find that page after page it takes us off guard, surprises us, and draws us into *its* reality, pulls us into participation with God on *his* terms" (p. 6).

The discipline of spiritual reading is "forbidding because it requires that we read with our entire life, not just employing the synapses in our brain" (p. 10).

"The danger in all reading is that words be twisted into propaganda or reduced to information, mere tools and data. We silence the living voice and reduce words to what we can use for convenience and profit" (p. 11).

"These words need rescuing" (p. 11).

Questions for Interaction

1. What is the Bible? How would you describe this famous book?
2. How many Bibles do you own? What kinds and translations do you have, and why?
3. In what ways do you find the Bible a difficult book to read?
4. Do you read the Bible on a regular basis? How often do you read it? How long? (This is not a contest!)
5. Do you "take your spiritual pulse" by the regularity of your Bible reading? In what ways might this be good and/or bad?
6. On a scale of 1 to 10, how well do you think you know the Bible? How do you think you could get to know it better?
7. How does a "manual for life" approach to the Bible reduce and distort it?
8. Peterson writes about "eating" the book, taking the Bible in and having it become a part of you. How does this approach to Scripture enhance and enlarge it?
9. How might your experience of Bible reading be different if you're trying to make a meal of it instead of reading it for helpful or inspiring bits?
10. Since eating is our primary metaphor for Scripture reading in this book, take some time to talk about the ways we eat and experience

food and drink. What descriptive words come to mind? Think of the way you approach eating an ice cream cone, a banquet, a snack, a humble breakfast, or other occasions for eating.

Suggested Activity

Eat a meal together. Divide up a psalm or some other passage and place cards with pieces of the passage at each seat. Over the course of the meal, have group members read from their cards (preferably in sequence). The group should feel free to talk as little or as much as they want about the passage, letting the conversation move back and forth between the actual meal, their daily lives, and the passage. Consider using this practice on a regular basis with your small group.

Prayer

For this first week, take the He section of Psalm 119 (verses 33-40) as your starting point for prayer.

> God, teach me lessons for living
>> so I can stay the course.
> Give me insight so I can do what you tell me —
>> my whole life one long, obedient response.
> Guide me down the road of your commandments;
>> I love traveling this freeway!
> Give me a bent for your words of wisdom,
>> and not for piling up loot.
> Divert my eyes from toys and trinkets,
>> invigorate me on the pilgrim way.
> Affirm your promises to me —
>> promises made to all who fear you.
> Deflect the harsh words of my critics —
>> but what you say is always so good.
> See how hungry I am for your counsel;
>> preserve my life through your righteous ways!

The Holy Community at Table with Holy Scripture

(pp. 15-22)

Summary

We are not in charge of shaping our own spiritualities. There is only one text for the creation of an authentic Christian spirituality, and that is Scripture. Over the centuries, despite numerous attempts to raise them to the level of Scripture, Christians have said "No" to ecstasy/enthusiasm, moral heroics, and emptiness/silence as "texts" for spirituality. As Peterson reminds us, "Christian spirituality is, in its entirety, rooted in and shaped by the scriptural text" (p. 15).

The preferred alternative "text" for spirituality today is the sovereign self, making "my life my authority instead of the Bible" (p. 16). The result is something self-centered instead of God-centered, with lots of zip instead of substance. But as Christians we take another road: "In contrast to the self-serving and glamorous spiritualities, ours is a pedestrian way, literally pedestrian: we put one foot in front of the other as we follow Jesus" (pp. 16-17). Being Christians means knowing Jesus and following in his way, and the Bible is what leads us into both.

Personal experience has its place, but it is under the authority of the Bible, not over it.

While there has been a renewed interest in the soul recently, there hasn't been a corresponding interest in the Bible. That leaves us foundationless and floating. "It is a matter of urgency," Peterson says, "that interest in our souls be matched by an interest in our Scriptures" (p. 17).

Scripture is revelation, words that reveal the Word that created, the Word that became flesh in Jesus for our salvation. But Scripture not only reveals God to us; it also invites us to participate in the life of God — with our whole lives. As Peterson points out, "The Bible, all of it, is *livable*; it is *the* text for living our lives" (p. 18). We don't stand at an objective distance from the Bible; we eat it, we take it in, "assimilating it into the tissues of our lives" (p. 20). Something changes in us when we eat food, and the same is true of eating Scripture. And we are changed not just individually but as the holy community of God, the church. As we engage Scripture as a community in various ways (not just through the Sunday sermon!), our identity in Jesus is restored, our lives are filled with the Spirit, and our discipleship is refreshed. Each of these things, constantly distorted or depleted by the surrounding culture, is revived.

Quotations to Consider

"God does not put us in charge of forming our personal spiritualities. We grow in accordance with the revealed Word implanted in us by the Spirit" (p. 15).

"The groundswell of interest in spirituality as this new millennium has opened up does not seem to be producing any discernable outpouring of energetic justice and faithful love, two of the more obvious accompaniments of a healthy and holy Christian life. In fact, we have arrived at a point now when the term 'spirituality' is more apt to call to mind dabblers in transcendence than lives of rigor, exuberance, goodness, and justice — the kinds of lives historically associated with this word" (p. 16).

"It is a matter of urgency that interest in our souls be matched by an interest in our Scriptures — and for the same reason: they, Scripture and souls, are the primary fields of operation of the Holy Spirit. An interest in souls divorced from an interest in Scripture leaves us without a text that shapes these souls" (p. 17).

"'Don't just take notes on the sermon. Eat the book'" (p. 19).

"The word 'book' . . . suggests that the message God gives to us has meaning, plot, and purpose. . . . God's word is written, handed down, and translated for us so that we can enter the plot" (p. 20).

"We do not come to God by guesswork: God reveals himself" (p. 20).

"The act of eating the book means that reading is not a merely objective act. . . . Readers become what they read" (p. 20).

"If Holy Scripture is to be something other than mere gossip about God, it must be internalized" (p. 20).

"Most of us have opinions about God that we are not hesitant to voice. But just because a conversation (or sermon or lecture) has the word 'God' in it, does not qualify it as true" (pp. 20-21).

"Come to the Table and eat this book, for every word in the book is intended to do something in us, give health and wholeness, vitality and holiness to our souls and body" (p. 22).

Questions for Interaction

1. How do you respond to the statement that the Bible is authoritative? Is it comforting? Stifling? Something in between?
2. How might ecstatic practices be enticing replacements for Scripture as the shapers of personal spiritualities? How might moral practices do the same? And self-emptying practices?
3. Some say that the single theme coming out of Hollywood for the past fifty years is "Follow your heart." How does this clash with the Bible as the one rooting and shaping text for Christian spirituality?
4. Are there ways in which pop psychology and self-help spiritualities replace the Bible in its role of shaping your life? Are you more familiar with psychological language or biblical? How would that affect your living?
5. Which tends to have the final word in how you live your life: personal experiences or Scripture? Why?
6. Scripture is not just for individual Christians but for the holy community. What role does Scripture play in the life of your church? Where, beyond the Sunday sermon, does it exert its influence in shaping your community?

Suggested Activity

Have three members of the group read the three "eating" passages from Scripture: Jeremiah in Jerusalem (Jer. 15:16), Ezekiel in Babylon (Ezek. 2:8–3:3), and John on Patmos (Rev. 10:8-10). Serve something sweet to eat with the Jeremiah and Ezekiel passages and then something bitter with the Revelation passage. Talk about both the sweetness and the bitterness of "eating" what God reveals in and through Scripture.

Prayer

Take the Mem section of Psalm 119 (verses 97-104) as your starting point for prayer. This section includes verse 103: "How sweet are your words to my taste, sweeter than honey to my mouth" (NIV); "Your words are so choice, so tasty; I prefer them to the best home cooking" (*The Message*).

> Oh, how I love all you've revealed;
> I reverently ponder it all the day long.
> Your commands give me an edge on my enemies;
> they never become obsolete.
> I've even become smarter than my teachers
> since I've pondered and absorbed your counsel.
> I've become wiser than the wise old sages
> simply by doing what you tell me.
> I watch my step, avoiding the ditches and ruts of evil
> so I can spend all my time keeping your Word.
> I never make detours from the route you laid out;
> you gave me such good directions.
> Your words are so choice, so tasty;
> I prefer them to the best home cooking.
> With your instruction, I understand life;
> that's why I hate false propaganda.

Scripture As Text: Learning What God Reveals

(pp. 23-36)

Summary

We are in process; our lives are being formed. Our experiences are important, but, as Peterson points out, "they are not the text for directing the formation itself" (p. 23). It's vital that we differentiate between text and context. Life and experience are the context, and thus we need to take them very seriously, but they are not the text. Scripture is the text. The text forms the context, not the other way around.

"Most, if not all, of what and who we are has to do with God. If we try to understand and form ourselves by ourselves we leave out most of ourselves" (p. 23). If God is the most important part of who we are, God-revealing Scripture is essential for knowing who we are and living well.

Our approach to Scripture can be informational (self-controlled) or formational (God-controlled). "In our reading of this book," Peterson says, "we come to realize that what we need is not primarily informational, telling us things about God and ourselves, but formational, shaping us into our true being" (pp. 23-24). The goal is not to *know* more, but to *become* more.

Scripture is revelation. In it, God is "not so much telling us something, but *showing* himself" (p. 24). However the words ended up on the pages, Christians have always held that God is responsible for them and intends them more for revelation than for information. "This is revela-

9

tion, personally revealed — letting us in on something, telling us person to person what it means to live our lives as men and women created in the image of God" (p. 24).

While the first Christians already had a complete, defined Bible (what we call the Old Testament), they gradually developed a sense that Paul's letters, the Gospels, and the few other parts of what became the New Testament had an "'authorial' continuity" with what they had first been given. The same author, the same Holy Spirit was at work in both bodies of writing. Yes, there were plenty of differences, but "the consensus that emerged was that embedded in all these differences and diversities there was a single voice and that this voice was personal, the voice of God revealing himself" (p. 26).

To account for the diverse expressions of the one voice, early Christians came up with the concept that is now called the Trinity. Not only did it express this united diversity within the revelation, but it expressed the relational nature of the revelation. Because this triune God is relational at his three-personed core, his revelation will be personal, drawing us personally into relationship. The Bible isn't just revelation — it is address. It is the voice of God speaking to us.

If the Bible is personal and relational in its revelation of the triune God, then it must also be read personally and relationally. It is to be listened to with a view toward participation — total participation. Because it reveals all of who God is and all of who we are, it calls for complete participation by both God and us. As we read and pray and live the text, our lives become congruent with it.

There are three approaches to Bible reading that let us escape a personal, comprehensive, relational reading: the intellectual, the practical, and the inspirational. Each has its benefits — Scripture offers much to think about, much to do, and much to feel — but each turns Scripture into a tool to be used for our own ends rather than recognizing it as the text that shapes us. Ironically, reading the Bible in these ways actually avoids dealing with God.

These approaches effectively replace the Trinity of Father, Son, and Holy Spirit with what Peterson calls the "replacement Trinity" of my Holy Wants, my Holy Needs, and my Holy Feelings. In this configuration, I am "a divine self in charge of my self" (p. 31). In a consumerist culture where "our tastes, inclinations, and appetites are consulted endlessly" and options proliferate, the imperial self is God. "If the culture does a thorough job on us,

. . . we enter adulthood with the working assumption that whatever we need and want and feel forms the divine control center of our lives" (p. 32).

The sacred texts of Holy Wants, Holy Needs, and Holy Feelings are these: "My needs are non-negotiable. . . . My wants are evidence of my expanding sense of kingdom. I train myself to think big because I am big. . . . My feelings are the truth of who I am" (p. 32). This "I" seeks to exorcise "the devils of boredom or loss or discontent — all the feelings that undermine or challenge my self-sovereignty" (p. 32).

The problem is that we can still read the Bible and feel good about ourselves while using it to support the idea that we, not God, are the sovereigns of our lives. This makes the imperative that we "eat this book" all the more urgent, since we must realize that God does not intend for us to use it for our own ends, as good as they may seem. Only by internalizing the revelation of Scripture will we truly know God and live well.

Quotations to Consider

"There is a sense in which we can never take ourselves too seriously. . . . But it is possible to conceive of ourselves too narrowly, for there is far more to us than our genes and hormones, our emotions and aspirations, our jobs and ideals. There is God" (p. 23).

"But here's the thing: every part of the revelation, every aspect, every form is *personal* — God is relational at the core — and so whatever is said, whatever is revealed, whatever is received is also personal and relational. There is nothing impersonal, nothing merely functional, everything from beginning to end and in between is personal" (p. 27).

"Christian reading is participatory reading, receiving the words in such a way that they become interior to our lives, the rhythms and images becoming practices of prayer, acts of obedience, ways of love" (p. 28).

"It is entirely possible to come to the Bible in total sincerity, responding to the intellectual challenge it gives, or for the moral guidance it offers, or for the spiritual uplift it provides, and not in any way have to deal with a personally revealing God who has personal designs on you" (p. 30).

"To put it bluntly, not everyone who gets interested in the Bible and even gets excited about the Bible wants to get involved with God" (p. 30).

"The new Trinity doesn't get rid of God or the Bible, it merely puts them to the service of needs, wants, and feelings" (p. 33).

"What has become devastatingly clear in our day is that the core reality of the Christian community, the sovereignty of God revealing himself in three persons, is contested and undermined by virtually everything we learn in our schooling, everything presented to us in the media, every social, workplace, and political expectation directed our way as the experts assure us of the sovereignty of self" (pp. 33-34).

"The blunt reality is that for all our sophistication, learning, and self-study we don't know enough to run our lives" (p. 34).

"Most of what we are told about God and his ways by our friends on the street, or read about him in the papers, or view on television, or think up on our own, is simply wrong. Maybe not dead wrong, but wrong enough to mess up the way we live" (p. 34).

Questions for Interaction

1. Peterson writes about the temptation to "understand and form ourselves" on our own — which we do at great cost to ourselves (p. 32). In what parts of your life are you tempted to understand and form yourself apart from God? What have the results been?
2. What is the difference between Scripture as "informational" and Scripture as "formational"? Which approach to Scripture do you usually take?
3. Do the scriptures of the New Testament feel to you like a continuation of the Old Testament by the same author? Why or why not?
4. Peterson calls the term "Trinity" a "construct" developed by the early Christians to explain what they saw to be true of God and of Scripture itself within the Bible. How does that help (or hurt) your understanding of God? Of Scripture?
5. How does the relational nature of the Trinity (Father, Son, and Holy Spirit in relationship with one another) give the revelation a relational nature?
6. Do you experience Scripture as the voice of God spoken to you? If not, how might your experience of Scripture be different if you did?

If you do, share a brief story of what this experience of Scripture is like for you.

7. People often avoid God's purposes in Scripture by using it for intellectual challenge, moral guidance, or spiritual uplift. Which of those three do you tend toward? How might it get in the way of receiving Scripture on God's terms?

8. Is your life in some ways governed by what Peterson calls "the new Holy Trinity"? In which ways do you bend Scripture to serve your Holy Wants? Your Holy Needs? Your Holy Feelings?

9. How well does it work when you (and others) allow your Holy Wants, Holy Needs, and Holy Feelings to become the authoritative "text" for your life? What does it do to community?

Suggested Activity

Play a song like Peter Gabriel's "Big Time" or Frank Sinatra's "My Way" or some other similar song (there are literally millions of "me-oriented" songs out there). Then talk about how our society feeds what Peterson calls our Holy Wants, Holy Needs, and Holy Feelings, and how this affects our Bible reading and our relationship with God.

Prayer

Take the Kaph section of Psalm 119 (verses 81-88) as your starting point for prayer.

> I'm homesick — longing for your salvation;
>   I'm waiting for your word of hope.
> My eyes grow heavy watching for some sign of your promise;
>   how long must I wait for your comfort?
> There's smoke in my eyes — they burn and water,
>   but I keep a steady gaze on the instructions you post.
> How long do I have to put up with all this?
>   How long till you haul my tormentors into court?
> The arrogant godless try to throw me off track,
>   ignorant as they are of God and his ways.

Everything you command is a sure thing,
    but they harass me with lies. Help!
They've pushed and pushed — they never let up —
    but I haven't relaxed my grip on your counsel.
In your great love revive me
    so I can alertly obey your every word.

Scripture As Form: Following the Way of Jesus

(pp. 37-58)

Summary

As useful as Bible reading is for the affirmation of doctrine, it is far, far better as a preparation for living. The goal of Bible reading is Bible living, Scripture in motion.

So how should we read Scripture? Peterson suggests the answer by comparing the Bible to a farm. He lived in farming country, he explains, and he couldn't recall a farmer who ever hurried. "Farmers characteristically work hard, but there is too much work to do to be in a hurry" (p. 39). Everything on a farm is connected; everything is in its context; everything has its place in larger rhythms. Hurrying, Peterson points out, only interrupts these rhythms. And much of what is going on is out of the farmer's control to begin with. So the farm teaches patience and attentiveness. Patiently and attentively (in other words, humbly), the farmer participates in the rhythms of the farm and the land. Like the farm, Peterson says, the Bible has its own rhythms that we must understand and respect. We can participate in them but not control them. This is the only kind of Bible reading that doesn't destroy the "ecology" of Scripture and soul.

The Bible is basically one big story, God's story. Our individual lives are stories within this story. Story is therefore the "primary verbal means of bringing God's word to us" (p. 40). There is more story in Scripture than anything else. And that's good, because the content of Scripture is more accessible that way. Like all good stories, it "doesn't just tell us something and leave it there, it invites our participation" (p. 40). It is neither sentimental and cute nor propagandistic and bullying.

Regrettably, we live in an age that prefers information to story. We tend to reduce stories to controllable information, which puts us outside of the story and in charge of it. We put ourselves in God's place instead of getting inside the story and participating in it. We reduce the text to information and then reduce ourselves by calling on experts to figure it all out for us.

What we are neglecting is the "'implicit invitation' to enter the story ourselves, just as we are, and discover for ourselves how we fit into it" (p. 42). The invitation comes from the biblical writers themselves, who don't tell too much. This leaves lots of room for us to enter into the narrative.

We don't have to change in order to become a part of the story, but we change as we participate in it. This is God's story, and he is moving it along — and everyone who participates in it.

Do we limit ourselves by focusing on this single story? On the contrary, says Peterson. We can go "traveling widely in Holy Scripture," since it is "the revelation of a world that is vast" (p. 45).

We are constantly tempted to either atomize or privatize the Bible. Pulling it apart by study techniques gives us lots of information but "replaces the adoring dalliance of a lover" (p. 46). On the other hand, in our attempts to personalize it, we often end up privatizing it, which amounts to stealing it from the community of Christ.

The story is the big thing in the Bible. The other forms of literature within the Bible are all embedded in the story. The larger story must be retained in all our readings of the smaller parts. The apparent contradictions in idea in Scripture are made coherent by the consistency of the meta-narrative, the meta-story, that holds it all together.

As we walk through Scripture, sentence by sentence, we don't want to focus so much on every step we take that we never get anywhere. But we also don't want to miss out on this wonderful territory by moving through it without sufficient awareness. Exegesis is what gives us the proper attentiveness to the text, enabling us to take in the details of the landscape of God in Scripture that we traverse.

Just as they have the ability to reveal, to draw us into a larger world, words also have the ability to conceal, to falsify and mislead. And words change: meanings and nuances are always in flux. This makes exegesis essential — but not easy. The difficulty of it tempts us to abandon it, to rely on our own intuitions and insight.

In the face of this temptation, we must remain committed to exegesis. The reading of biblical commentaries should become common practice for common Christians, not just sermon-writers.

As Peterson says, "Exegesis is loving God enough to stop and listen carefully to what he says" (p. 55). This listening involves submitting to the text, not mastering it. In this way, "exegesis is an act of sustained humility" (p. 57).

Key Terms

Meta-story: A large, sprawling story that gathers other stories into it. The story of God — from creation to salvation to new creation — is one large, sprawling story that gathers our smaller life stories into it. Our lives find meaning and shape within the larger narrative of God's story, just as the smaller events of our lives find meaning and purpose within the larger narrative of our lives.

Exegesis: "Exegesis is the discipline of attending to the text and listening to it rightly and well" (p. 50). It requires the self-control of listening to what the text actually says and the restraint of not trying to make it say what it doesn't say, especially if that's what we want it to say. Rather than a scholarly pursuit, it is the process of humbling ourselves to Scripture (something not necessarily associated with scholarship).

Quotations to Consider

"The Bible turns out to be a large, comprehensive story, a *meta-story*. The Christian life is conducted in story conditions" (p. 40).

"Honest stories respect our freedom; they don't manipulate us, don't force us, don't distract us from life" (p. 41).

"When we submit our lives to what we read in Scripture, we find that we are not being led to see God in our stories but our stories in God's. God is the larger context and plot in which our stories find themselves" (p. 44).

"When we privatize Scripture we embezzle the common currency of God's revelation" (p. 46).

"The Bible, the entire Bible, is 'relentlessly narratival.' And we cannot change or discard the form without changing and distorting the content" (p. 47).

"Many of us have picked up the bad habit of extracting 'truths' from the stories we read" (p. 48).

"It takes the whole Bible to read any part of the Bible" (p. 48).

"All our masters in spirituality were and are master exegetes. There's a lot going on here; we don't want to miss any of it; we don't want to sleep-walk through this text" (p. 50).

"Exegesis is foundational to Christian spirituality. Foundations disappear from view as a building is constructed, but if the builders don't build a solid foundation, their building doesn't last long" (p. 53).

"The more mature we become in the Christian faith, the more exegetically rigorous we must become. This is not a task from which we graduate" (p. 53).

"Without exegesis, spirituality gets sappy, soupy. Spirituality without exegesis becomes self-indulgent. . . . And prayer ends up limping along in sighs and stutters" (p. 58).

Questions for Interaction

1. How does God's story get us back in touch with our lives, our souls?
2. The Scriptures "seek to subject us." How do we become subject to God's will by becoming subjects in God's story?
3. The biblical writers leave a lot of blanks in their stories, inviting us to participate in them. For instance, St. Paul never gives details about his "thorn in the flesh" (2 Cor. 12:7). How does this help you enter into the story?
4. Have you ever heard people talk about "welcoming" or "inviting"

God into this or that part of their lives? How does this get the story backward? Who is the main character in that case? How does this mess up our participation in God's story?

5. At what points in your life have you engaged in "decorator spirituality," using "God as enhancement" to your life? What role has Scripture played in helping you move from using God in your life to entering into the life and story of God?

6. Peterson talks about "traveling widely in Holy Scripture" (p. 45). What does he mean by this? How widely have you traveled in Scripture? Where haven't you traveled much, if at all?

7. What is the difference between personal and private? How can we hear ourselves personally addressed by Scripture and yet not privatize it?

8. What kinds of stories are escapist entertainment, pulling us out of our lives, out of God's story? What kinds of stories take us deeper into both?

9. If the Bible is "relentlessly narrative," what does that tell us about the way we should express it — in preaching, in theology, in teaching, in praying?

10. Peterson says spirituality without exegesis ends up "sappy," and prayer ends up "limping along" (p. 58). How can we, personally and communally, sustain an emphasis on exegesis?

Suggested Activity

One of the features of the Ignatian spiritual exercises is the invitation to enter into the stories in the Gospels with all five senses. Read aloud the story of the wedding at Cana from John 2 and invite the group to close their eyes and enter into the story with their senses:

- taste the first wine and then Jesus' wine
- hear the sounds of the party: the music, the conversation, Jesus' word to Mary
- feel the sun and the breeze
- smell the perfume and the burning wax of the candles
- see the colorful clothing of the wedding guests and the looks on their faces

Discuss how a sensual entering into the text can open up both the meaning of the text and your own lives in response to what Jesus says and does.

Prayer

Take the Waw section of Psalm 119 (verses 41-48) as your starting point for prayer.

> Let your love, God, shape my life
>   with salvation, exactly as you promised;
> Then I'll be able to stand up to mockery
>   because I trusted your Word.
> Don't ever deprive me of truth, not ever —
>   your commandments are what I depend on.
> Oh, I'll guard with my life what you've revealed to me,
>   guard it now, guard it ever;
> And I'll stride freely through wide open spaces
>   as I look for your truth and your wisdom;
> Then I'll tell the world what I find,
>   speak out boldly in public, unembarrassed.
> I cherish your commandments — oh, how I love them! —
>   relishing every fragment of your counsel.

Scripture As Script:
Playing Our Part in the Spirit

(pp. 59-77)

Summary

Our cultural context is not conducive to good Bible reading. Taught from a young age to take charge of our lives, many of us take charge of Scripture instead of submitting to its authority over us. Ironically, we do this despite the fact that we believe in Scripture's authority.

In this context of control, we often talk of "applying" Scripture, as if it were like paint applied to a house or a Band-Aid put on a wound — always exterior. But Scripture is really something far larger than we are, a world that we enter and are shaped by, not some external "thing" that we add to our lives and conform to our purposes.

We learn Scripture primarily through our feet (our obeying), not through our ears (our hearing). Our reading is completed in our living. God speaks by telling a story, and we listen in order to participate in it. Receptivity, imagination, and participation are required of us.

But the Bible isn't always congenial. St. John got a stomachache after he ate it, and we have a similar experience: what first tastes sweet to us ends up being bitter and hard to take. This happens because, as Peterson points out, "the book is not written to flatter us, but to involve us in a reality, God's reality, that doesn't cater to our fantasies of ourselves" (p. 64). Bible reading is hard, not just because it can be difficult, but because it can be painful to hear and obey. The Bible doesn't "behave" the way we'd like it to. Our temptation is to domesticate it, to repair it, to sand off the edges to get it to do what we want it to do. When we reduce Scripture to palatable concepts, we try to ignore and dispense with uncomfortable details.

Scripture tells us and shows us that God is doing something new and creative. That's the good news. The bad news is that we have to give over control to get in on it. We don't get God into our lives; we get into God's life. We read the Bible to meet God, not to get stuff for ourselves, no matter how "spiritual" that stuff is.

The world of the Bible corresponds to God, not to us. Like the God it reveals, it is staggering in its immensity. We need revamped and enlarged imaginations in order to take it in. Our experience is far too small to contain it; "it's like trying to fit the ocean into a thimble," Peterson says (p. 68). The smaller worlds of our lives are taken into and find their place in the expansive universe of Scripture.

In a world filled with lies and manipulations, we've learned a "hermeneutics of suspicion," a refusal to take things we read at face value. And this is important, because it protects us against those who would take advantage of us. But after our suspicion has allowed us to dispense with all the junk we encounter, we need to come to Scripture with a "second naiveté" so that we can bring a "hermeneutic of adoration" to reading it.

All Bible reading is for the sake of following Jesus. It all funnels into obedience — or it's supposed to. "Obedience is the thing, living in active response to the living God. The most important question we ask of this text is not, 'What does this mean?' but 'What can I obey?'" (p. 71). It's not so much that knowing the text leads to obeying it, but that obeying it leads to knowing it. Participation begets a desire for more.

Peterson reminds us that the Bible must be read liturgically — not in the specific sense of what goes on in a Sunday-morning service, but in a much larger sense: we must read Scripture as part of the whole Christian community throughout the world and down through the ages. Liturgy in this sense gathers the community together in worship and then sends us out to lives of mission. With its emphasis on community, liturgy keeps us from privatizing the Bible. The Bible is *our* book; liturgy helps us to respond *together*.

When we "eat this book" and internalize it the way a skilled musician internalizes a piece of music, it expresses itself freshly and spontaneously in the details of our lives, in a "virtuoso spirituality." Without it, "unscripted," we stutter anxiously through life, out of tune and out of rhythm.

Quotations to Consider

"We are in the odd and embarrassing position of being a church in which many among us believe ardently in the authority of the Bible but, instead of submitting to it, use it, apply it, take charge of it endlessly, using our own experience as the authority for how and where and when we will use it" (p. 59).

"Language is not primarily informational but revelatory. . . . This text is not words to be studied in the quiet preserve of a library, but a voice to be believed and loved and adored in workplace and playground, on the streets and in the kitchen. Receptivity is required" (p. 62).

"This book makes us participants in the world of God's being and action; but we don't participate on our own terms. We don't get to make up the plot or decide what character we will be" (p. 66).

"We enter this text to meet God as he reveals himself, not to look for truth or history or morals that we can use for ourselves. . . . We do not read the Bible in order to find out how to get God into our lives, get him to participate in our lives. That's getting it backward" (p. 67).

"We've learned to our sorrow that religious people lie more than most others — and lies in the name of God are the worst lies of all" (p. 68).

"Liturgy is the means that the church uses to keep baptized Christians in living touch with the entire living holy community as it participates formationally in Holy Scripture" (p. 73).

"The task of liturgy is to order the life of the holy community following the text of Holy Scripture" (p. 73).

"Liturgy preserves and presents the Holy Scriptures in the context of the worshipping and obeying community of Christians who are at the center of everything God has done, is doing, and will do. The liturgy won't let us go off alone with our Bibles, or self-select a few friends for Bible study and let it go at that" (p. 74).

"Liturgy keeps us in touch with the story as it defines and shapes our beginnings and ends, our living and dying, our rebirths and blessing in this Holy Spirit, text-formed community, visible and invisible" (pp. 74-75).

Questions for Interaction

1. What's the difference between applying something (e.g., a Band-Aid to a scratch) and eating something? Why do you think Peterson prefers the image of eating Scripture to the image of applying Scripture?
2. The Hebrew word *shema'* means both "to hear" and "to obey." How often does your hearing of Scripture lead to an obeying of it? Why is there often a gap between the two?
3. What does it mean to listen to the story of the Bible with imagination?
4. Have you ever been in a Bible study or heard a sermon (or given one!) in which the text was explained away so that the group or preacher could get to what they really wanted to talk about in the first place? What's going on in this kind of situation? Why do we behave this way?
5. What would happen to you if you gave up control over the story of your life and instead entered into the story God is writing?
6. Do you treat the Bible as an addition to your life? What if, instead, your life were added to that story?
7. In C. S. Lewis's *The Lion, the Witch and the Wardrobe*, four children pass through a small wardrobe to discover a large and astonishing world. How does Bible reading compare to that experience?
8. Does your Bible reading lead to obedience, to following Jesus? What gets in the way of obedience?
9. What sets the rhythms of your year, your life? How heavily is it shaped by things like school, work, holidays, paydays, vacations, department-store sales? What about the liturgical church year? What would it look like to live a life shaped by the rhythms of Scripture and worship and community?

Suggested Activity

Take a large bedsheet and a thimble. Tell the group that the thimble is their life and the sheet is God's life. Try squeezing the sheet into the thimble. Then place the thimble inside the sheet. Talk about the difference between inviting Jesus into our cramped lives and thanking him for inviting us into his spacious life (and story).

Prayer

Take the Lamedh section of Psalm 119 (verses 89-96) as your starting point for prayer.

> What you say goes, God,
>   and stays, as permanent as the heavens.
> Your truth never goes out of fashion;
>   it's as up-to-date as the earth when the sun comes up.
> Your Word and truth are dependable as ever;
>   that's what you ordered — you set the earth going.
> If your revelation hadn't delighted me so,
>   I would have given up when the hard times came.
> But I'll never forget the advice you gave me;
>   you saved my life with those wise words.
> Save me! I'm all yours.
>   I look high and low for your words of wisdom.
> The wicked lie in ambush to destroy me,
>   but I'm only concerned with your plans for me.
> I see the limits to everything human,
>   but the horizons can't contain your commands!

SESSION 6

Caveat Lector

(pp. 81-89)

Summary

Reading the Bible can be wonderful. If we take it in the right way, our lives are permeated by the revelation of God.

But it can also be dangerous. "Let the reader beware," Peterson urges (p. 82). Handled incorrectly, it easily becomes a weapon, just as deadly as a car driven poorly. And having a Bible nicely bound and bought and in our hands gives us the feeling of being in control. We can read as we choose, recite and use passages as we choose.

How we read the Bible is easily as important as what we read in it. The goal of our reading is to live appropriately before God. Reading that departs from that goal quickly becomes dangerous. Instead of just talking about the text, which is always a temptation, we need to live by its words. "Live what you read," Peterson says (p. 84).

Peterson reminds us that words written are dead words, just ink on a page, no longer living as they were when spoken. But the words of Scripture are words awaiting resurrection by the Spirit — just as the Word himself was resurrected.

Peterson also reminds us that we have the words of the Bible, not the world of the Bible, not their original context. The practice of *lectio divina* is something that can help us recover that context. This practice cannot be confined to those times that we are studying Scripture; it is "a way of life that develops 'according to the Scriptures.' It is not just a skill that we exercise when we have a Bible open before us but a life congruent with the Word made flesh to which the Scriptures give witness" (p. 89). *Lectio divina* is what keeps us from reducing the Word of God, what helps us work it deep into our thinking, working, relating, worshipping lives.

Quotations to Consider

"The Christian community is as concerned with *how* we read the Bible as *that* we read it" (p. 81).

"The words printed on the pages of my Bible give witness to the living and active revelation of the God of creation and salvation, the God of love who became the Word made flesh in Jesus. . . . If in my Bible reading I lose touch with this livingness, if I fail to listen to this living Jesus, submit to this sovereignty, and respond to this love, I become arrogant in my knowing and impersonal in my behavior" (p. 82).

"An enormous amount of damage is done in the name of Christian living by bad Bible reading" (p. 82).

"We read the Bible in order to live the word of God" (p. 84).

"Words written are radically removed from their originating context, which is the living voice" (p. 85).

"Many of us prefer words written to words spoken. It is simpler, we are more in control, we don't have to deal with the complexities of difficult, neurotic, or insufferably boring people" (p. 87).

"Speaking comes first. Writing is derivative from speaking. And if we are to get the full force of the word, God's word, we need to recover its atmosphere of spokenness" (p. 87).

"There is a sense in which the Scriptures are the word of God dehydrated, with all the originating context removed. . . . We are left with the words of the Bible but without the world of the Bible" (p. 88).

"It is the task of *lectio divina* to get those words heard and listened to, words written in ink now rewritten in blood" (p. 89).

Questions for Interaction

1. Briefly recount an occasion when someone used the Bible danger-ously, either as a weapon or without proper responsibility. Are there ways in which you have used the Bible dangerously?
2. Is there something you have believed, thinking that it was what the Bible said, only to discover later that the Bible didn't say that at all?
3. Have you ever been in a Bible study where people wanted to talk about the text but weren't very interested in living it? What went wrong? What can we do to make sure that our reading is less to *in-form* us than to *form* us and the way we live?
4. Since we never truly leave our particular context (gender, national-ity, denomination, personal history, etc.), how can we keep it from contaminating the way we approach the words of Scripture?
5. How can we enter the context in which the words of Scripture were written so that we hear them as they were intended to be heard?

Suggested Activity

Have a group member read aloud the first chapter of Revelation. Talk about the "spokenness" and specific context of the chapter — the blessing on the one who reads; the blessing on those who "listen"; the setting of St. John on Patmos; the setting of the seven churches in Asia Minor, who would be reading what he wrote. How would all of these things affect the reading/hearing of what follows? How might a purely contemporary read-ing distort what follows? How might reading what follows as mere infor-mation kill the "livedness" that our reading is supposed to bring?

Prayer

Take the Heth section of Psalm 119 (verses 57-64) as your starting point for prayer.

> Because you have satisfied me, God, I promise
> to do everything you say.
> I beg you from the bottom of my heart: smile,

be gracious to me just as you promised.
When I took a long, careful look at your ways,
  I got my feet back on the trail you blazed.
I was up at once, didn't drag my feet,
  was quick to follow your orders.
The wicked hemmed me in — there was no way out —
  but not for a minute did I forget your plan for me.
I get up in the middle of the night to thank you;
  your decisions are so right, so true — I can't wait till morning!
I'm a friend and companion of all who fear you,
  of those committed to living by your rules.
Your love, God, fills the earth!
  Train me to live by your counsel.

SESSION 7

"Ears Thou Hast Dug for Me"

(pp. 90-117)

Summary

Welcome to the meat of the book. Everything has led up to this and will flow out of this. This is where we learn in depth about the most appropriate kind of Bible reading: not self-justifying, not controlled, but done in company, reconnected, storied, personalized, listened to, responded to, lived — *lectio divina*.

While they have a natural progression, the four elements of *lectio divina* are not sequential. They grow together in a more organic way. That only makes sense, because this is reading that becomes a way of living.

Lectio means "read." More particularly, *God speaks and we listen.*

How do we listen well, read well? By avoiding literal reading, which tends to be surface reading — taking Scripture at face value alone. The Bible is full of metaphors, of "true lies," and understanding metaphor keeps us from the trap of literalism. We need metaphors because all language is inadequate, especially language applied to God. (When the word "awesome" is used to describe a bathroom cleaner as well as God, we know we're in trouble.) Reading metaphors as metaphors opens up our imagination, inviting us to step into God's story. The literal lie of a metaphor jars us out of literalist language, engaging the imagination and enabling

30

words to say more than they usually say. Metaphors defy systematic theology but welcome personal participation.

Metaphor is necessary because of the collision between the transcendence (otherness, distance) of God and our experience of his immanence (withness, interaction, nearness). There is a huge gap, *and* there is a powerful experience of proximity — both. The lie of the metaphor expresses the gap, and the concreteness of the metaphor expresses the proximity. Metaphors lead to reverential engagement.

***Meditatio* means "engage."** *God speaks and we listen, finding ourselves personally engaged.*

Written words speak but can't be spoken to. Written words can be spoken against but can't speak back. In other words, they are words removed from personal speech and specific context. That's why it's so essential to re-engage Scripture in a conversation.

"Meditation moves from looking at the *words* of the text to entering the *world* of the text," Peterson explains. "As we take this text into ourselves, we find that the text is taking us into itself. For the world of the text is far larger and more real than our minds and experience" (p. 99). Scripture will always be larger than we are because God is its context. Meditation moves us into the "More" of the revealed God, keeping us from reducing him to a usable "Less."

According to Peterson, many of us today fragment Scripture into something like the Sibylline Oracles, breaking it into chunks of biblical "wisdom" that we can insert into our lives without ever entering into the life of God revealed in Scripture. The division of the Bible into chapters and verses, which makes for easy navigation and memory, encourages this approach. Meditation does the opposite. It brings us into the story. "Meditation enters into the coherent universe of God's revelation. Meditation is the prayerful employ of imagination in order to become friends with the text" (p. 101).

Meditation helps us make the move from being outside the text, using it, to being inside the text, living it. "Meditation is participation" (p. 102).

***Oratio* means "pray."** *God speaks and we listen, finding ourselves personally engaged and in need of responding in prayer.*

God wants more than just our listening. He wants our responding.

He wants a relationship. God speaks and gives us the gift of speech. We speak to the God who speaks to us.

Our central and best guide is found right in the middle of our Bibles: the book of Psalms. The Psalms teach us how to pray in response to God's revelation. The Psalms are an "anatomy of the soul," showing us that any and every part of our lives can and should be prayed, especially the dark parts. The Psalms also show God from a variety of angles, giving us a more complete picture of him than any of our experiences alone ever could.

If the Psalms are "our primary text for prayer," Peterson says, "then Jesus, the Word made flesh, is our teacher" (p. 106). In the Lord's Prayer we find a brief but powerful guide to prayer. But more important than what Jesus teaches us is the fact that he is praying for us — right now.

In order to understand Scripture — God's Word to us — we have to understand prayer — our words to God. The two are like salt and pepper, never to be separated. When we get this connection, we discover that Scripture isn't really God's *speech* to us. It's the beginning of God's *conversation* with us.

Prayer has never been easy. It wasn't easy for Jesus when he was in Gethsemane or on the cross. But "God didn't say it would be easy," Peterson reminds us (p. 108). And prayer has the power to move us from our small lives into the larger life of God. It's difficult, but it's rewarding.

***Contemplatio* means "live."** *God speaks and we listen, finding ourselves personally engaged and in need of responding in prayerful living.*

Contemplation "ties worship in the sanctuary and work in the world in a bundle that is at once secular and sacred" (p. 110). Contemplation isn't the work of super-spiritual people in undistracted places; it is the work of all Christians all the time. It is simply living in the presence of the God revealed in Scripture. It is therefore a life lived in protest against all the other reduced and manipulated versions of life that we're handed by our culture.

"Contemplation means submitting to the biblical revelation, taking it within ourselves, and then living it unpretentiously, without fanfare," Peterson says (p. 112). It is not a sign of having "arrived" spiritually: "All contemplatives are failed contemplatives" (p. 113).

In the everyday world, a word like "contemplation" is uncommon. We need an uncommon word like this not because we're an uncommon people, but because we're doing an uncommon thing: uniting the word read with the word lived. Not living the word that we read, using it but not living it, is diabolical. Keeping what we read in the realm of ideas instead of in our lives is devilish.

Unlike the other three elements of *lectio divina*, contemplation is less a human action than an action of the Spirit, God working his word read, engaged, and prayed into the fabric of our lives. It is not a technique to be mastered, but a way of attending to and responding to God.

Quotations to Consider

"*Lectio divina* is a way of reading that becomes a way of living" (p. 91).

"The psalms poet was bold to imagine God swinging a pickax, digging ears in our granite blockheads so that we can hear, really hear, what he speaks to us" (p. 92).

"Print technology — a wonderful thing, in itself — has put millions and millions of Bibles in our hands, but unless these Bibles are embedded in the context of a personally speaking God and a prayerfully listening community, we who handle these Bibles are at special risk. If we reduce the Bible to a tool to be used, the tool builds up calluses on our hearts" (p. 92).

"Reading is always preceded by hearing and speaking. . . . Just because we have read it, doesn't mean we have heard it" (p. 92).

"Meditation is the aspect of spiritual reading that trains us to read Scripture as a connected, coherent whole, not a collection of inspired bits and pieces" (p. 100).

"Every word of the scriptural text is a window or door leading us out of the tarpaper shacks of self into this great outdoors of God's revelation . . ." (p. 102).

"Prayer is language used in relation to God. It is the most universal of all languages" (p. 103).

"It is a wonder that God speaks to us; it is hardly less a wonder that God listens to us. The biblical revelation is equally insistent on both counts:

the efficacy of God's language to us, the efficacy of our language to God. Our listening to God is an on-again, off-again affair; God always listens to us. The essential reality of prayer is that its source and character are entirely in God" (p. 104).

"The Scriptures are our listening post for learning the language of the soul, the ways God speaks to us; they also provide the vocabulary and grammar that are appropriate for us as we in our turn speak to God" (p. 104).

"Prayer is *engaging* God, an engaging that is seldom accomplished by a murmured greeting and a conventional handshake. The engagement, at least in its initial stages, is more like a quarrel than a greeting, more like a wrestling match than a warm embrace" (p. 105).

"In prayer anything goes. . . . Nothing human is excluded. The Psalms are an extended refutation that prayer is 'being nice' before God" (p. 105).

"In prayer we are most ourselves; it is the one act in which we can, *must*, be totally ourselves. But it is also the act in which we move beyond ourselves" (p. 107).

"God does not make speeches; he enters conversations and we are partners to the conversation" (p. 107).

"Contemplation means living what we read, not wasting any of it or hoarding any of it, but using it up in living. It is life formed by God's revealing word, God's word read and heard, meditated and prayed" (p. 113).

"It is astonishing how many ways we manage to devise for using the Bible to avoid a believing obedience, both personal and corporate, in receiving and following the Word made flesh" (p. 117).

Questions for Interaction

1. The first step in reading the Bible well is understanding metaphor. What are some of your favorite biblical metaphors for God (examples: rock, shepherd, vine)? How does the imprecise nature of these metaphors open up your understanding of God? How do metaphors keep that understanding personal and not wooden?

34

2. Are there ways in which you use the Bible like the Sibylline Oracles, giving fragments of wisdom without providing a story or a context? Is it common practice to use the Bible that way in your church?

3. What is the danger of memorizing Bible verses without concern for context? How might Scripture be memorized in a way that helps hold its story together?

4. Does the Bible feel more like a bunch of odd pieces stuck together or a connected whole? What makes it feel one way or the other?

5. Do you ever get the sense that God is speaking to you in Scripture? How do you respond?

6. How has Bible reading increased the kinds of prayers you pray? How has it changed the kinds of things you say in your praying?

7. According to Peterson, the Psalms teach us that prayer isn't "being nice" before God, that anything goes. What sorts of feelings or topics do you tend to avoid when you pray? How do the Psalms open up previously "unprayed areas" of your life?

8. More important than our own praying is Jesus praying for us (which he is doing at this very moment). How does the fact that Jesus is praying for you (right now) free you up to pray with less guilt or anxiety?

9. What do you find hardest about prayer?

10. What do you think of when you hear the word "contemplation"? Is it positive or negative? Does it entice you or make you want to go to sleep? Is it a word you would use of yourself or of other people?

11. Peterson says that a child intently watching an ant trek across a log is engaged in contemplation. What mundane activities in your life might be contemplative? How might they be places where God's word, heard and prayed, gets lived?

12. Have you seen your life become shaped by Scripture over time? Where have you seen it in the other members of your group?

Suggested Activity

Collect a variety of images — perhaps a few dozen — that are used of God throughout Scripture (e.g., groom, king, gardener, shepherd, hen, lion, tower, etc.). Give group members copies of these images, or project them onto a screen. Have the group reflect personally and together on how the images expand their understanding and experience of God and keep them from reducing God to a short list of abstract qualities.

Prayer

Take the Qoph section of Psalm 119 (verses 145-152), which draws on the solidity of God and his Word in the midst of shaky times, times of suffering.

> I call out at the top of my lungs,
>   "God! Answer! I'll do whatever you say."
> I called to you, "Save me
>   so I can carry out all your instructions."
> I was up before sunrise,
>   crying for help, hoping for a word from you.
> I stayed awake all night,
>   prayerfully pondering your promise.
> In your love, listen to me;
>   in your justice, God, keep me alive.
> As those out to get me come closer and closer,
>   they go farther and farther from the truth you reveal;
> But you're the closest of all to me, God,
>   and all your judgments true.
> I've known all along from the evidence of your words
>   that you meant them to last forever.

SESSION 8

God's Secretaries

(pp. 121-36)

Summary

The Bible is the most translated book in the world. Translations of the Hebrew scriptures were made long before Jesus was born. Aramaic replaced Hebrew as the spoken language of the Jews during the Exile, requiring the first translations. (There are bits and pieces of Aramaic in both the Old and New Testaments.)

Because of linguistic and geographic and political changes, the Hebrew scriptures had been shelved until the return of the exiles and the ministry of Ezra the priest and Nehemiah the politician. Nehemiah united the people politically; Ezra reconnected the people with the biblical story. At first Ezra tried reading them the story in the original Hebrew. But because they had become disconnected with the biblical language, the people needed some interpretive help to understand the Scriptures. So Ezra had thirteen Levites interpret and explain to the people the "sense" in Aramaic of what he was reading. What the Levites said did more than engage the minds of the people; it engaged their lives by expressing the text's meaning in everyday language.

Two hundred years later, Alexander the Great conquered the world linguistically as well as militarily, and the everyday language throughout the Mediterranean world became Greek. The Jews were now dispersed throughout this land, and more and more of them came to speak Greek.

This explains why the first complete translation of the Hebrew scriptures was a Greek translation (called the LXX or the Septuagint). Dispersed as they were, with no land to call their own, the Jews needed their Holy Scriptures — "the only soil left to them," Peterson calls it (p. 128) — in a language they could understand.

Peterson describes the legend that developed about how the Hebrew scriptures were translated. But, legend aside, the people of God believed that the same Spirit that was at work in the initial writing and compiling of the Scriptures was also at work in the translating of them.

Peterson concludes this chapter by telling his own modern-day story of translation. As an American pastor, he found that he was much like the Levites, "giving the sense" of the text to a congregation unfamiliar "with their past, with their Scriptures, their biblically formed identity" (p. 130). And then something happened that made them retreat, made them become fearful and distrustful — not what Christians are called to be. When Peterson saw this — his congregation living lives that obviously weren't being shaped by God and the story of God revealed in Scripture — he decided to become a more thoroughgoing translator himself. He chose to translate Galatians for them because he thought it was the message they most needed. The translation had to be done in American, in the kind of language that they used at home, in school, and at work. It had to be in the language of their lives in order to get into their lives. It was out of this pastoral need that the translation that became *The Message* originated.

Quotations to Consider

"The overwhelming majority of men and women who have heard and/or read the word of God as revealed in Scripture and by proclamation have done it with the help of a vast company of translators" (p. 121).

"This is the intended end of true translation, to bring about the kind of understanding that involves the whole person in tears and laughter, heart and soul, in what is written, what is said" (p. 125).

"The significance of the *Letter* [the story about the translation of the Bible into Greek] for us is the enormous respect and honor in the Jewish (and later Christian) community that was given to this translation and its translators. They believed that the same Spirit of God at work in the writing of Scripture is also at work in the translating of Scripture" (p. 129).

"For both Jews and Christians the original and the translation were on a par with one another as authoritative Scripture" (p. 130).

"And then something happened that without my being aware of its significance at the time put me in the company of translators" (p. 131).

"I tried to imagine Paul as pastor to these people who were letting their hard-won freedom in Christ slip through their fingers. . . . I had no plan, no program, nothing ambitious like Greek. I just wanted them to hear it the way I heard it, the way the Galatians heard it, the way Luther heard it, the way so many men and women through our Christian centuries have heard it and found themselves set free by and for God" (p. 134).

"Without knowing what we [the adult church-school class] were doing, or the impact it would make on our culture, we had joined the company of translators, 'God's secretaries'" (p. 135).

"When I sat down with the Hebrew and Greek texts to translate them into American for the congregation beyond my congregation, it didn't seem all that different from what I had been doing for thirty-five years as a pastor. . . . I was always aware as a pastor that I was required to be neighborhood-specific. Generalities and 'big' truths would not do" (p. 136).

Questions for Interaction

1. Think of times in your life when the grand promises of the Bible seemed the farthest thing from your lived experience. The same was true for the biblical characters. Were you able to reconcile the gap between promise and experience? If so, how?
2. Have there been times when you've become disconnected with the biblical story? If so, what helped you reconnect with the story?
3. Do the foreign languages in which the Bible was originally written — Hebrew, Aramaic, and Greek — make it feel inaccessible to you? What helps make the Bible more accessible to you?
4. When the Jewish people were spread across the Roman empire,

they were no longer rooted in the soil of the holy land. Holy Scripture was their soil. How does the Bible provide a solid soil in which you can root your life? How does it connect you with other Christians in other times and places and conditions?

5. In what ways is a translator like a prophet?
6. How might some translations keep people from reading the Bible? What might be done about that?
7. What do you believe is more important: that a translation be exact or that it be readable? Why?
8. Does your pastor or Bible-study leader translate the Bible into your everyday language? How might having someone you know and trust translate Scripture help you read and digest it?

Suggested Activity

Get as many translations of the Bible as possible and look at some favorite passages together. (There are many online Bibles. One web site that has many translations collected and is easily searchable is www.biblegateway .com.) Discuss how the slight differences between them might cause confusion on the one hand and might bring added depth and revelation and joy on the other.

Prayer

Take the Pe section of Psalm 119 (verses 129-136) as your starting point for prayer.

> Every word you give me is a miracle word —
>   how could I help but obey?
> Break open your words, let the light shine out,
>   let ordinary people see the meaning.
> Mouth open and panting,
>   I wanted your commands more than anything.
> Turn my way, look kindly on me,
>   as you always do to those who personally love you.
> Steady my steps with your Word of promise

so nothing malign gets the better of me.
Rescue me from the grip of bad men and women
    so I can live life your way.
Smile on me, your servant;
    teach me the right way to live.
I cry rivers of tears
    because nobody's living by your book!

SESSION 9

The Message

(pp. 137-76)

Summary

Jesus spoke the language of God in the language of the people he inter-acted with. Not only was he God made flesh, but he made the word of God flesh too.

At its intended best, "we use language to reveal to one another who we uniquely are. We are not just using words to exchange information . . . but *revealing ourselves*: revealing our hopes and dreams, our thoughts and prayers, that vast interiority that we summarize as *soul*, this unfathom-able mystery of who we are as 'image of God'" (p. 138). But language is easily defiled, downward or upward. Defiled downward, it is used to re-duce or manipulate or desecrate. Defiled upward, it is used to flatter or distance or deal with ideas instead of people.

The goal of Bible reading isn't the reading of a sacred text, Peterson reminds us. It's having our lives shaped by the reality of the God who has revealed himself to us through the text. Our reverence for the text more often than not gets in the way of our reading, engaging with, praying, and living the Scriptures — it keeps us from *lectio divina*. When that happens, it's time to get a new translation.

We also need a new translation when the language of the text we're using doesn't resonate with our everyday language. Peterson's case in point is the King James Version and the series of revisions it has undergone. "Even though the revisions have provided us with an impressively accurate text, they have not prevented a continuously widening gap between the language of the Bible and the language we use in our everyday lives" (p. 141). But we have been rescued by two important archaeological discoveries.

The first, an archaeological discovery in Oxyrhynchus in Egypt in 1897, transformed New Testament translation. In a garbage dump in that city, two men discovered Greek writing on some discarded scraps of paper. Among the words they discovered were almost all of the words that had been assumed to be "'Holy Ghost' words" (p. 145), language found in the New Testament that wasn't found in great Greek literature and therefore was deemed especially spiritual. It turned out to be street speech. It wasn't opera; it was rap. This was everyday speech without an ounce of pretension in it.

With a few exceptions, the New Testament wasn't written in special speech. It was written in the speech of the poor and working class that Jesus loved so much. It wasn't polished; it was accessible.

But there have been many attempts to elevate the Bible, spiritualizing its earthy language and message. Origen and others did it to the "daily bread" of the Lord's Prayer. The translators for the King James Version did it to William Tyndale's translation, taking what had been readable by a plowboy and elevating it to a form of language no one spoke.

The second archaeological discovery, made in Ugarit in Syria in 1923, involved thousands of inscribed clay tablets. When translated, the tablets, Peterson says, "provided a detailed accounting of the culture that the Hebrews encountered and were immersed in upon arriving in Canaan" (p. 153). But while Israel shared the same language and cultural forms as the Canaanites, it was never overpowered by them. And "while they used the same literary forms, the content was radically different" (p. 154) — faithful to the biblical history, not caught up in the fanciful myths and sex-and-religion paganism around them.

The Oxyrhynchus and Ugarit discoveries have uncovered our tendency to remove the text of Scripture from our everyday lives. Our problem isn't that our translations are inaccurate; they are very accurate. Our problem is that nobody talks that way. That's where *The Message* comes in. It recovers the language of the everyday.

Language isn't as cut-and-dried as we'd like it to be. It's filled with ambiguity and allows for all sorts of misunderstanding. Because of that, a

literal translation is almost always inadequate. It can tell you what someone said in a wooden way, but it can actually distort what they mean by
doing so. "We need a familiarity with the 'life' that is being translated," Peterson says; "but we also require a familiarity with the 'life' into which it is
being translated" (p. 169).

Martin Luther called the critics of his translation "lemmings." Peterson says that literalism "lobotomizes" language, killing any imagination
in the original text and in the language it's translated into. Sensitive translation, on the other hand, which inevitably involves paraphrase, elaborates and enriches God's word. Peterson tells us that "his first experience
with paraphrase" (p. 173) came when he was in high school: he read J. B.
Phillips's paraphrase of the New Testament Epistles. That gave him more
than Scripture to study; it gave him a Bible he could eat, he says, a Bible
that got inside of him, shaping his imagining and his living. And eventu-
ally, when he joined "the company of translators," it shaped his writing of
The Message.

Quotations to Consider

"Language is sacred at its core. It has its origin in God" (p. 137).

"*Having* and *defending* and *celebrating* the Bible instead of *receiving, submitting
to,* and *praying* the Bible, masks an enormous amount of nonreading"
(p. 140).

"The translators . . . noticed that the Greek of Paul and Mark was quite different from the Greek they had learned in the schools. The Greek of the
New Testament sounded so barbarous to the educated that it had to be
defended by the early church" (p. 143).

"All those special words that occurred nowhere else in written records,
those 'Holy Ghost' words, were all the time buried in a town garbage
dump, preserved under Egyptian sand. They were all street words, spon-
taneous, unstudied expressions out of the immediacy of workplace and
kitchen" (p. 145).

"When Augustine first read the Bible he was greatly disappointed. . . . It
was only after his conversion that he realized that this word of God was
not an elevated language used by philosophers and poets to discourse on

the 'higher things' but the language in which men and women were finding themselves addressed by the Holy Spirit in the thick of everyday life" (pp. 151-52).

"Jesus is the *descent* of God to our lives just as we are and in the neighborhoods in which we live, not the *ascent* of our lives to God who we hope will approve when he sees how hard we try and how politely we pray" (p. 152).

"The culture of Israel doesn't come to us in a pure state. . . . The scriptural revelation and life of salvation did not develop in isolation from their Canaanite neighbors" (p. 154).

"While the Hebrews were perfectly at home in Canaanite culture in one sense, willing and able to use the language and adapt its forms, they were also practiced in discernment. They knew how to say 'no' to the culture when they had to" (p. 155).

"These are the stories [the God-stories of the Hebrews] that formed Israel's imagination — quiet, everyday, the supernatural camouflaged in the natural, the presence of God revealed in the places and among the people involved in our day-to-day living. The entire biblical text stands in sturdy contrast to the myths of Ugarit — but also to the potpourri of religious psychology, self-development, mystical experimentation, and devotional dilettantism that provides the textual basis for so much contemporary religion" (p. 160).

". . . the first people who heard or read the Bible didn't need a dictionary or a concordance" (p. 166).

"Each language is an intricate and living culture. . . . If all we are translating is dictionary meanings, the entire culture is lost in translation" (pp. 169-70).

"Translation is betrayal. All translation is inherently mistranslation. Each language is unique. The particular genius of a language cannot be carried over into another" (p. 170).

"Preference for the literal has a long life. But I have come to believe that it is an unthinking preference. . . . The peril of the literal is that it ignores the inherent ambiguities in all language, takes the source language prisoner and force-marches it, shackled and chained, into an English that nobody living speaks. The language is lobotomized. . . . Extreme literalism insists on forcing each word into a fixed immovable position, all the sentences strapped into a straitjacket" (p. 171).

"Rather than diluting the pure word of God, each new translation elaborates it" (p. 172).

"Translation is interpretation. Always. It is interpretation because words always convey far more meaning than the dictionary assigns them" (p. 173).

"I wanted to convey by means of American syntax and diction that everything in this book [the Bible] is livable, that the most important question is not 'What does it say?' but 'What does it mean and how can I live it?'" (pp. 175-76).

Questions for Interaction

1. What are some ways that you've heard the language defiled downward (used to desecrate or reduce or manipulate) this past week? Don't just think of instances of profanity; consider things like advertisements too.
2. What are some ways that you've heard the language defiled upward (used to flatter or distance or "functionalize" others) this past week?
3. In what ways does the too-sweet talk of "Christianese" distance us from God and others? Give some examples.
4. Which do you find easier to read: the Bible or the newspaper? Why?
5. What keeps you from reading the Bible?
6. Does the translation of the Bible you read sound like a sacred text or like the language of your life? Explain why.
7. How does a new translation bring new life to your encounter with God in Bible reading?
8. Peterson writes, "Israel shared the Canaanite language and culture without being overpowered by it" (p. 154). How can we do the same? How can our reading of Scripture enable us to be fully American while being uniquely Christian?
9. How are the stories about sports, movie, and rock stars like the myths of Canaanite gods and goddesses? How are the simple, spare

stories (e.g., the story of Abraham and Sarah) in which God truly acted like our humble lives? Which shapes your imagination more?

10. Share a story in which someone — child, student, employee — has used the literal meaning of something you said in order to get out of doing what you really meant. Are there ways in which you've done the same thing with what God means in Scripture?

Suggested Activity

Imagine what it would have been like before there was a Bible: hearing stories about David for the first time, or the twenty-first time, around the evening fire; listening to one of Paul's letters read in its entirety to the church that met in your home. How might you hear this pre-Scripture differently? What barriers would this build up or knock down in your ability to receive it as God's revelation?

Now try one of the two settings above. If it's warm enough outside, try meeting around a fire (if possible) and telling stories about David or Jesus from memory (you'll want to refresh your memory first!). If it's cold or wet outside, meet in a small, intimate space if possible. Tell your group that they are the church in Philippi and that you've just received a letter from their brother Paul, who is in prison, and that you're eager to read it to them. Then read the whole epistle straight from *The Message*.

Prayer

Take the Taw section of Psalm 119 (verses 169-176) as your starting point for prayer for your final session.

> Let my cry come right into your presence, God;
> > provide me with the insight that comes only from your Word.
> Give my request your personal attention,
> > rescue me on the terms of your promise.
> Let praise cascade off my lips;
> > after all, you've taught me the truth about life!
> And let your promises ring from my tongue;
> > every order you've given is right.

Put your hand out and steady me
    since I've chosen to live by your counsel.
I'm homesick, God, for your salvation;
    I love it when you show yourself!
Invigorate my soul so I can praise you well,
    use your decrees to put iron in my soul.
And should I wander off like a lost sheep — seek me!
    I'll recognize the sound of your voice.